Series 561

FLORENCE NIGHTINGALE

by L. DU GARDE PEACH, M.A., Ph.D., D.Litt.

with illustrations by JOHN KENNEY

Publishers: Ladybird Books Ltd . Loughborough
© Ladybird Books Ltd (formerly Wills & Hepworth Ltd) 1959
Printed in England

FLORENCE NIGHTINGALE

The name of Florence Nightingale is known all over the world, and honoured in every civilised country. Because of her life's work, sick people are to-day properly cared for in thousands of hospitals and nursing homes.

Florence's father was a rich man, and it was whilst her parents were living in Florence, Italy, in 1820, that their daughter was born. This is why she was christened Florence.

They soon returned to England, and Florence grew up to be a rather solemn little girl. She was very fond of playing with her dolls, and her favourite game was to pretend that they were sick, and that she was nursing them back to health.

At the same time she learnt from her father a great deal about the way England was governed, and with her mother she used to visit sick people in the little town of Romsey near which she lived, taking food and medical comforts.

One day Florence was out riding on her pony in the company of the parson of a near by church. As they rode across the common, they saw an old shepherd sitting by the roadside with his sheep-dog, Cap, beside him.

The shepherd was very fond of his dog, and was bitterly bemoaning the fact that it had met with an accident. Its leg was broken, and it looked as though poor Cap would have to be destroyed.

When she heard this, Florence jumped down from her pony, and together with the parson, examined the dog's broken leg. They made splints for it and bandaged it up, and soon the dog was running about again, as well as ever.

The shepherd was very grateful to Florence, and when she became the most famous nurse in the world, he used to tell people that her first patient had been his dog, Cap.

When Florence grew to be a young woman, her love of dolls changed to an interest in people and all the new and exciting things which were happening in England. Her father had been High Sheriff of Hampshire, and many famous men used to come to their house, including Lord Palmerston, afterwards Prime Minister.

It was a time when England was changing from a country mostly of farms to one of big cities and factories. Railways were being built, and such inventions as the telegraph were changing peoples lives.

Florence had an inquiring mind, and was interested in seeing things for herself. This led her one day to visit a hospital, and she suddenly realised that here was something which needed doing, and which she could do.

The hospital she saw, like all the hospitals in those days, was dirty and badly run. The nurses knew nothing about how to look after sick people, and few of those who had to go into hospital expected to come out alive.

At that time nursing was not the great profession which it is to-day, and Florence's parents were horrified when she told them that she wanted to become a nurse. They did all they could to prevent their daughter from doing something which they thought was not fit for an educated young lady.

For years Florence tried in vain to get them to agree. In the meantime, she studied all the books on medicine which she could get, and devoted herself to nursing her relations when they were ill. As she had nine uncles and aunts, most of whom had children, she had plenty of practice.

At last, when she was thirty, Florence persuaded her parents to let her go to Germany and Paris to study nursing, and for four years she worked hard at the profession she had chosen.

Then something happened which was to change her whole life. The Crimean War broke out.

The Crimean War was in 1854, when Florence was thirty-four years old. It was fought between Russia on one side, and Turkey, helped by England and France, on the other.

The southern part of Russia, called the Crimea, is a long way from England. When our soldiers were sent there, no one really knew what the weather and the country were like. Our soldiers suffered a great deal because they only had their summer uniforms in a climate which was very cold in winter. Also, everything which was sent out to them had to go in sailing ships, which were very slow, and were often wrecked on the way.

The English soldiers fought very bravely, and soon won the first battle of the war, the Battle of Alma.

This was called after the River Alma, and was fought only six days after the English troops landed in the Crimea. They crossed the river and charged up the hill on the other side, where the Russians were entrenched. Soon the hill was captured and the Russians retreated to a town called Sebastopol.

A large number of English soldiers had been wounded at the Battle of Alma, and they had to be taken back first to the coast, and then by sea to the hospitals at Scutari.

To-day every country has ambulances and medical services to look after wounded soldiers in time of war. But in 1854 there were no ambulances, and the wounded men had to be taken across very bad roads in rough carts. Many of them died of their wounds on the way.

The people in England would have known nothing about these things if there had not been, in the Crimea, a man sent there by " The Times " newspaper. He saw all that was going on, and he wrote in his paper about the condition of the English wounded. He said " Our men were sent to the sea, three miles distant, on jolting carts. The French had covered hospital vans, and their wounded were sent in much greater comfort than our poor fellows ".

When the wounded soldiers at last arrived at Scutari, the hospitals to which they were sent were not at all like the hospitals of to-day. They were old buildings, dirty and practically falling down, and because there were not enough beds, wounded men were lying all over the floor.

Often the men had no blankets, and because there were very few doctors, it was sometimes days before their wounds were attended to. Many of the soldiers died who would have lived if they had been properly cared for.

There were, of course, no nurses in the English hospitals, and the wounded men must have envied the French who had much better hospitals, attended by French nuns.

The correspondent who had written to " The Times " about the carts visited the hospitals at Scutari, and he sent a despatch back to England in which he said: " Are there no devoted women amongst us able and willing to nurse the sick and suffering soldiers in the hospitals of Scutari?"

The Minister of War in England was a man called Sidney Herbert, and when he read about the state of the hospitals in Scutari he decided that nurses should be sent out to them. He already knew Florence Nightingale, and he wrote a letter to her.

" There is only one person in England that I know who would be capable of organising such a scheme. Would you listen to the request to go out and organise the whole thing?"

Florence had not waited for Sidney Herbert's letter. She also had read about the condition of the hospitals at Scutari, and on the very same day she had written offering to go. Two days later she went to see Sidney Herbert at the War Office.

Everything was quickly arranged, and in less than a week Florence was officially appointed Superintendent of the nurses to be sent out to the English hospitals.

The immediate task before her was to find nurses who were suitable and who were ready to go.

Florence had a close friend named Mrs. Bracebridge who offered to go with her and help her. So when Florence began to interview nurses who were willing to join, she had Mrs. Bracebridge at her side.

An office was opened in London, and soon there were a great many women waiting to be interviewed. It had been decided only to take forty, but even though hundreds of women volunteered, it was very difficult to select the right ones.

Many of the women were rough and ignorant, and had never had any training. Others were well educated women who thought it would be romantic to look after wounded soldiers, but who had no idea of what it was really like in a military hospital.

After seeing many hundreds of women, Florence finally selected thirty-eight. Most were devoted nurses from religious hospitals.

Florence Nightingale did not waste any time. She thought always of the suffering men at Scutari, and knew that the sooner she and her nurses could get there, the more lives would be saved. Within a week of offering to go, she and her nurses were ready to embark on the ship for the long voyage.

Although a great many people in England thought that Florence Nightingale was being both brave and patriotic, there were others who were scornful. They said that women could not stand the bad weather in Turkey, and that instead of nursing the wounded soldiers, they would all become ill and require nursing themselves.

When this little party of brave women left London there were no cheering crowds, as there had been when the soldiers marched away. People looked on coldly and said that they would soon be back again.

But Florence Nightingale and her nurses took no notice. They were doing what they knew to be their duty.

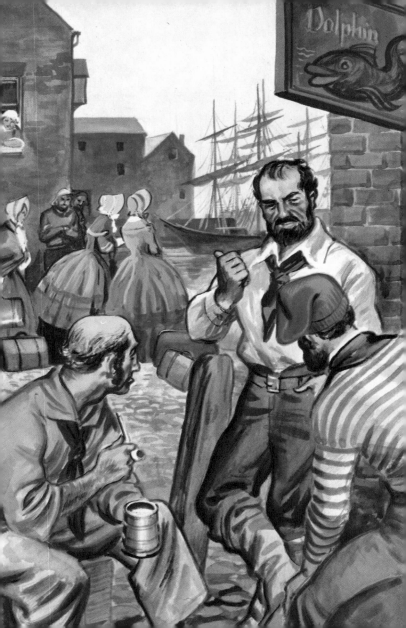

Instead of sailing across the Bay of Biscay and into the Mediterranean by way of Gibraltar, the party of nurses travelled across France to Marseilles. When they arrived at Boulogne, on the other side of the English Channel, a wonderful welcome awaited them.

The French crowds cheered them as heroines, and people fought to be allowed to carry their luggage. Wherever they went they were given everything they needed. When they stayed at hotels, the hotel-keepers would not let them pay anything, and even the French railways insisted that they should travel free.

All this meant very little to Florence Nightingale. Her one desire was to get to Scutari as soon as possible. She knew that soldiers were dying for want of the care which she and her nurses could give them. She was happy when the journey across France was over, and they were all aboard the " Vectis " for the voyage to the East.

It was at the end of October that Florence Nightingale and her nurses left France, and the Mediterranean can be very rough at that time of the year. No sooner had they got clear of the land than a great storm blew up.

They were in a sailing ship, and soon several of the sails had been torn from the yards by the force of the wind. The ship was in great danger of going on the rocks.

Added to this, many of the nurses were sea-sick, and soon they were regretting that they had ever volunteered to come.

A fortunate change in the wind made it possible for the ship to get into harbour at Malta. Here they sheltered until the storm ceased and the sea became calm. Then they set sail again, and arrived at Scutari eight days after leaving Marseilles.

In the meantime, whilst Florence and her nurses were still at sea, another battle had been fought in the Crimea; the Battle of Balaclava.

This was the name of a village which was held by English and Scottish soldiers, together with a few hundred Turks. The Russians attacked it, and were only stopped by the bravery of the British cavalry.

The Battle of Balaclava is famous in British history because of the charge of the Light Brigade. This was a force of about six hundred mounted men. Because of a mistake about what they were supposed to do, these six hundred men galloped along a valley more than a mile long, with Russian cannon shooting at them from all sides.

A great many of them were killed and wounded, but they never stopped until they had ridden right up to the cannon and captured them.

A great English poet, Lord Tennyson, has written a poem describing this famous charge.

The wounded soldiers from the Battle of Balaclava were arriving at the hospitals at Scutari as the "Vectis" sailed into harbour. But instead of the army doctors welcoming Florence Nightingale and the nurses she had brought, they were all against her.

These old army doctors were afraid that women would upset the hospitals and alter all their arrangements. This was just what Florence Nightingale was determined to do when she saw how dirty and badly run the hospitals were.

Dr. John Hall was the chief army doctor. As he could not order Florence to take her nurses back to England, he decided to make them so uncomfortable that they would very quickly go back of their own accord. He arranged for them to live in an old, ruined tower, overrun with rats, and without any heating or furniture.

Dr. Hall did not know that Florence Nightingale was one of the most determined women who ever lived. She had come to Scutari to nurse the wounded, and nothing he could do would stop her.

The rooms in the hospital, called the wards, were in a terrible state. It is no wonder that Dr. Hall did not want the trained nurses from England to see them. They were horribly dirty and wounded men were put into the same wards as men with infectious diseases. There were not enough blankets or beds, and the food was badly cooked and usually cold before the men got it.

In spite of everything Dr. Hall could do or say, Florence put the nurses to work at once, scrubbing the floors, washing the bedclothes, and making the wounded men comfortable.

The soldiers were grateful, but the doctors continued to make things as difficult as possible for the nurses. They realised that if they had done their duty properly, the nurses would not have had to scrub and clean the wards. They were afraid that reports might be sent back to England by Florence to her friend, the Minister of War.

Florence was too busy to send reports back to England. All she wanted to do was to make the hospitals clean and comfortable.

Soon there was a very great improvement. Instead of wounded men lying anywhere and everywhere on the filthy floor, and even in the corridors, they were in clean beds in properly disinfected wards. This had a very good effect on the patients. As soon as they felt that they were being looked after and cared for, they began to get better.

In a very few days men who had been in the depths of misery and despair, hoping only to die, were sitting up, cheerful and happy.

The hospitals at Scutari had disgraced the name of Britain; now, because of the devoted work of a few women, they were better than those of the French which the English soldiers had been envying ever since the war started.

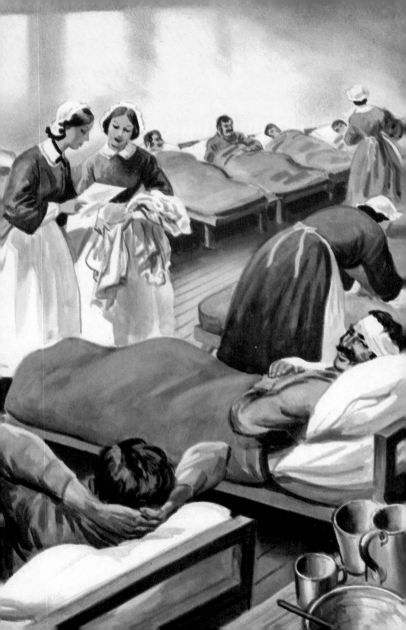

Dr. Hall was a very unpleasant man. Instead of thanking Florence for all that she had done, he was bitterly jealous of her. The soldiers hated him for the way in which he had neglected them, and he saw how grateful they all were to the gracious lady who had given them hope and courage.

But although Florence Nightingale's devotion had failed to win even the most grudging recognition from Dr. Hall, the younger doctors realised the difference she had made to the hopes and prospects of the wounded. They were more generous than their cross-grained chief.

The nurses had proved that the people in England were wrong who doubted whether they were suitable for nursing wounded soldiers in war. From that day women nurses have always been part of the Army, and in two world wars many thousands of wounded soldiers have owed their lives to them.

A hundred years ago the British Army was very different from the Army of to-day. Soldiers were sent to the war in the Crimea from places like India, wearing the thin summer uniforms which are suitable for hot climates. But the Crimea was bitterly cold in winter, and the Army had not arranged for any warm clothing to be sent out from England.

Boots were also sadly needed by the soldiers, and there was great rejoicing when it was learnt that a shipload of boots was on its way from England. Unfortunately, when it arrived, it was found that all the boots were for the left foot.

Florence set herself to remedying this state of things. She bought warm clothing and distributed it to the soldiers, and during the first few months she supplied. ten thousand shirts which the Army was quite unable to provide.

At the same time Florence and her nurses took over the hospital kitchens, and from then on the wounded men got good hot food, properly cooked.

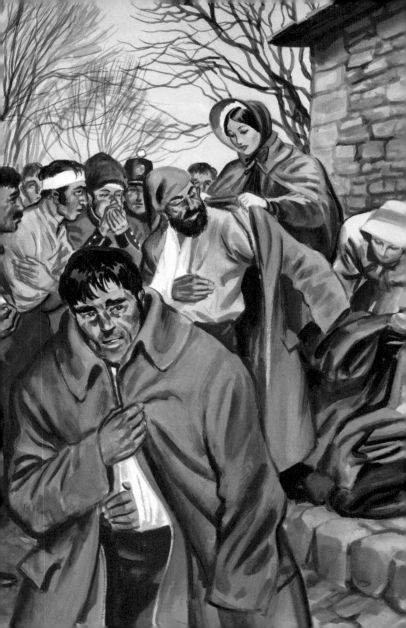

Although Florence Nightingale's name was now known to everybody, and she was honoured everywhere for the wonderful work which she was doing in the Crimea, Dr. Hall hated her as much as ever.

He knew that the more she did, the more people at home would realise how much he had neglected to do. He complained that Florence was making the soldiers so comfortable in the hospitals that they did not want to leave them. His idea was to make the hospitals so uncomfortable that the men would be glad to go back to the fighting line.

Then one day Dr. Hall sent for Florence and angrily told her that she was doing more harm than good, and that she must take her nurses back to England.

Florence did not argue with him. Instead, she showed him a letter which she had that day received from Queen Victoria, thanking "Miss Nightingale and her ladies" for all that they were doing.

Dr. Hall had nothing to say.

Florence took good care to ensure that everybody saw the letter from the Queen. The result was that nobody dared to stop her from doing what she knew to be right for the wounded.

When a hospital is full of hundreds of wounded men, such things as bandages and medical supplies of all sorts are needed in large quantities. There never seemed to be enough, and then one day Florence discovered that there were large stores of all these things which Dr. Hall would not allow her to have. He said that they could not be issued until a committee had agreed to release them.

When Florence was told that the committee would not meet for another three weeks, she was very angry. Men were suffering for lack of these very stores.

So Florence and her nurses broke open the boxes whilst Dr. Hall and the committee looked on horrified. They would have liked to interfere, but they remembered the letter from Queen Victoria.

Although the food given to the men in the hospitals at Scutari was now better cooked than it had been, it was still lacking in variety. For one thing, green vegetables were not to be had, and without green vegetables people are very liable to become ill.

Florence decided that it would be a very good thing when Spring came, to plant green vegetables in the waste land surrounding the hospitals. So she persuaded two wounded sergeants to dig up some of the ground for the planting of lettuces and cabbages.

Soon they were surrounded by groups of men very much amused at seeing sergeants digging in the warm Spring sun. They thought it was a great joke, until Florence herself appeared. Within minutes they all had their coats off and were digging beside the sergeants.

Dr. Hall was furious, but the wounded got green vegetables, and recovered all the quicker because of them.

Florence Nightingale was always a woman who wanted to see for herself. She was also a woman with a great talent for organising things so that they worked smoothly. In fact on one occasion Queen Victoria said of her " I wish we had her at the War Office".

When wounded men continued to arrive at Scutari, still with the dirt of the battle-field on them, and with their wounds either badly dressed or not dressed at all, she decided to go to Balaclava and inspect the first line dressing stations. Of course, Dr. Hall tried to stop her, but as usual he failed.

So Florence went right up into the Crimea, only just behind the trenches round Sebastopol. Here she was received not by jealous and incompetent doctors, but by men who owed their lives to her, and others who knew that if they were wounded, she would care for them.

As she drove round in her little carriage, the troops cheered her as though she were the Queen.

Back at Scutari, Florence once more devoted herself to the work of improving the hospitals and nursing the wounded. She found that things were now more difficult for her, because her friend, Sidney Herbert, was no longer Minister for War.

But she still had the support of the Queen and the devotion of the soldiers. The Queen had written to her again, and in the letter she had said " You are, I know, well aware of the high sense I entertain of the Christian devotion which you have displayed during the war. I need hardly repeat to you how warm my admiration is for your services, which are fully equal to those of my brave soldiers "

As for the soldiers themselves, there are no words strong enough to express their devotion.

In the night hours, sometimes long after midnight, Florence used to walk through the quiet wards to see that all was well, carrying a little lamp to light her way. Such was their love for her, rough soldiers used to kiss her shadow as she passed.

Florence Nightingale's work in the Crimea was done, and the end of the war brought her back to England.

When she had sailed in the " Vectis " only two years earlier, no one had been there to see her off, except those who sneered at her for going. Now, on her return, she was received by a nation which hailed her as the greatest woman of her time.

She was called the Angel of the Crimea, *The Lady of the Lamp*, and everywhere she went people crowded the streets to see her pass and to do her honour.

The great moment came when she was received by Queen Victoria and given a diamond brooch, designed by the Prince Consort, with " Crimea " and " Blessed are the merciful " engraved upon it.

Florence Nightingale will always be famous among the great women not only of England, but of the world. The efficient hospitals and devoted nurses of to-day owe an immortal debt to her, and through them the lives of all of us have been affected by the work of this great and gracious lady.

Series 561